Saint André Bessette

Miracles in Montreal

Written by Patricia Edward Jablonski, FSP

Illustrated by Barbara Kiwak

Pauline
BOOKS & MEDIA
Boston

Library of Congress Cataloging-in-Publication Data

Jablonski, Patricia E.

Saint André Bessette : miracles in Montreal / written by Patricia Edward Jablonski ; illustrated by Barbara Kiwak.

p. cm. -- (Encounter the saints series)

ISBN 0-8198-7140-0 (pbk.)

1. André, Brother, Saint, 1845-1937--Juvenile literature. 2. Christian saints--Canada--Biography--Juvenile literature.   I. Kiwak, Barbara. II. Title.

BX4700.A443J33 2010

282.092--dc22

[B]

2010031637

Cover art/Illustrated by Barbara Kiwak

All rights reserved. No part of this book may be reproduced or transmitted in any form or by any means, electronic or mechanical, including photocopying, recording, or by any information storage and retrieval system, without permission in writing from the publisher.

"P" and PAULINE are registered trademarks of the Daughters of Saint Paul.

Copyright © 2010, Daughters of Saint Paul

Published by Pauline Books & Media, 50 Saint Pauls Avenue, Boston, MA 02130-3491

Printed in the U.S.A.

STAB VSAUSAPEOILL09-10J10-06820 7140-0

www.pauline.org

Pauline Books & Media is the publishing house of the Daughters of Saint Paul, an international congregation of women religious serving the Church with the communications media.

1 2 3 4 5 6 7 8 9   14 13 12 11 10

Encounter the Saints Series

Saint Francis of Assisi
Gentle Revolutionary

Saint Ignatius of Loyola
For the Greater Glory of God

Saint Isaac Jogues
With Burning Heart

Saint Joan of Arc
God's Soldier

Saint John Vianney
A Priest for All People

Saint Juan Diego
And Our Lady of Guadalupe

Saint Katharine Drexel
The Total Gift

Saint Martin de Porres
Humble Healer

Saint Maximilian Kolbe
Mary's Knight

Saint Paul
The Thirteenth Apostle

Saint Pio of Pietrelcina
Rich in Love

Saint Teresa of Avila
Joyful in the Lord

Saint Thérèse of Lisieux
The Way of Love

CONTENTS

1

Smiles and Tears

Isaac Bessette waited impatiently. When would the midwife let him in? A baby's feeble cry finally broke the silence. Then, "Isaac . . . where's Isaac?" The nervous father hurried to his wife's bedside. "I'm here, Clothilde," he softly reassured her. "Everything is all right. Rest now."

But things were far from right. The midwife cradled a whimpering baby boy in her arms. She fixed her gaze on the tiny form. "He seems very ill, Clothilde," she murmured. "Shall I baptize him for you? If he lives, you can take him to the priest. He will do what can't be done now in an emergency."

"Yes, please! Do it right away," the exhausted mother cried. "If my child is not to stay with us, I pray that he will go straight back to God. At least he will have been baptized."

That night seemed endless. Clothilde and Isaac worriedly hovered over their baby. They watched and prayed. By the next day, August 10, 1845, the crisis had passed.

Joy filled the one-room cabin on the outskirts of the Canadian village of Saint-Grégoire.

"It's time to bring baby Alfred into town," Isaac happily notified his brother Edouard and sister-in-law Josephine. They would be the godparents. Because there was no permanent church in Saint-Grégoire, the ceremony was held in a building that served as a schoolhouse and meeting hall. That was where the local pastor offered Mass on a portable altar every Sunday. Father Sylvestre completed the Rite of Baptism. He blessed the baby, anointed him with chrism, and wrote his name in the baptismal record book. Alfred Bessette was now not only a child of God, but also an official member of the Catholic Church.

Little Alfred was born with a serious stomach problem. It bothered him all his life. Even though foods such as white bread, fruits, vegetables, and meat were expensive, Mr. and Mrs. Bessette made sure that Alfred always had whatever he needed.

Isaac Bessette was a hard worker, but the times were not the best. All of the Bessette children did what they could to help earn money. Isaac, a carpenter by trade, often took his older sons with him to cut trees from the nearby forest for timber. When he was old enough, Alfred would beg, "Papa, can't I come with you today?" But his father's answer was always the same. "Your mother needs you at home. You're the man of the house while your brothers and I are away." It was a kind way of saying that Alfred was too frail and small to help with the lumbering work.

Two more children were born to Mr. and Mrs. Bessette after Alfred. That brought the total to ten. Young Alfred was very happy to be surrounded by such a large and loving family. After all, it was fun to have so many brothers and sisters to play with! The Bessette family lived a simple but joyful life. They loved to sing together, especially in the evenings when the day's work was done. Every night, the family also prayed the Rosary together. Alfred would sit by his mother's side and finger her beads along with her. "My mother was always smiling," he would remember years later. "She had such a lovely smile." Alfred also recalled his mother's devotion to the saints. "She's the one who gave me my devotion to Saint Joseph."

When Alfred was ten, an unexpected tragedy changed his family's life forever. One blustery day in February 1855, Mr.

Bessette and his older boys went out to cut down some trees. Not long after they left, there was a frantic knock at the door. Mrs. Bessette opened it to find a solemn-faced neighbor. The man nervously wrung his cap in his hands. "Clothilde," he began, "I have some very bad news . . . There's been a terrible accident . . ."

"An accident? Where? How? No—no it can't be my Isaac!" Mrs. Bessette wailed.

"A tree fell on him, Clothilde," the neighbor quietly explained. "The men are bringing him home now. Your sons are with them. You'd better call the doctor. I'll . . . I'll be praying for you all."

The doctor arrived soon after Isaac was carried in on a makeshift stretcher. "I'm so sorry, Mrs. Bessette," he said after examining Isaac. "There is nothing I can do for him. It will be best to send for the priest . . ."

The pastor came and administered the last sacraments. By the next day, Isaac Bessette had gone to meet God.

Clothilde tried her best to provide for her children. But the effort proved to be greater than her strength. She soon came down with tuberculosis of the lungs—a serious disease. Clothilde had to send her children to live with friends and relatives

"Clothilde, there's been a terrible accident..."

who could care for them. She kept only Alfred with her. The two of them had always had a special relationship, and he needed more care because of his poor health. Alfred and his mother moved to the town of Saint-Césaire. There they lived with Marie-Rosalie, Clothilde's sister, who was married to Timothée Nadeau.

Clothilde worried that Alfred was not getting an education. He could never attend classes in the village school for more than a week without getting sick. This left him far behind the other children his age. Between Alfred's physical weakness and his mother's illness, little could be done. So at the age of twelve, he still couldn't read or write.

Clothilde Bessette fought her dreaded disease courageously for two years. But in those days, there were no antibiotics to treat people with tuberculosis. In the late fall of 1857, Clothilde died. She was just forty-three years old.

Alfred was heartbroken. Now he was an orphan. *What should I do, Lord?* he prayed. *What's going to happen to me?*

2

CHANGES

Mr. Nadeau, Alfred's uncle, expected the young boy to do his share of work around the house and farm as his own five children did. But it soon became clear that Alfred was simply too weak to do even minimal farm work. "Rosalie, I've heard the town cobbler needs some help," Mr. Nadeau casually mentioned one evening. His wife looked up from her knitting. "Do you think Alfred could do that type of work?" she asked.

"It's worth a try," her husband responded. "In the morning, I'll speak to the cobbler."

Soon enough, young Alfred became an apprentice cobbler. He learned how to make and repair shoes. Alfred was happy to earn a salary. He wanted to help his aunt and uncle. Unfortunately, even this new job was too much for his strength. After a few months, his Aunt Rosalie couldn't help noticing how sickly and pale Alfred looked. "This job isn't good for him, Timothée," she told her husband. "We'll have to find him something else."

Alfred next went to work for a baker. But that didn't turn out well either. His uncle finally agreed to give him lighter work around the farm. The local farmers sometimes hired Alfred for part-time jobs too, always giving him the easier chores.

The happiest event of Alfred's life during this time was his first Communion. Father André Provençal, the pastor of the village of Saint-Césaire, helped Alfred to prepare himself to receive Jesus. He also shared with him his own great devotion to Saint Joseph. Now that Alfred was working, he felt closer and closer to Saint Joseph, who had worked so hard to provide for Jesus and Mary.

In April of 1860, Alfred's uncle Timothée decided to join the "gold rush" to California. Before leaving, he moved his family to the village of Farnham. Fifteen-year-old Alfred was hired as a worker on the Ouimet farm on the outskirts of the village. Mr. Ouimet gave Alfred a crucifix. The boy hung it in the barn. Every evening after his long workday, Alfred would spend time kneeling before that crucifix. He and Jesus understood each other. They were very good friends.

Weeks passed. Alfred tried his best on the farm, but he just wasn't cut out to be a farmhand. His efforts ended in failure. He became an apprentice again, working first with a tinsmith, then with a blacksmith. But every job he tried ended in disaster because of his poor health. He finally ended up being taken in by a kind priest named Father Springer. The priest allowed him to live in the rectory in exchange for doing chores around the church.

I need to find a real *job,* Alfred told himself one day. *I can't stay here forever. I have to find my place in the world.* So, when he was twenty years old, Alfred decided to look for work in the United States. He spent three years working in mills and factories in Connecticut and other parts of New England, where many French-speaking Canadians had immigrated. He even learned to speak English. Still, Alfred struggled. He was a poor laborer in a foreign country. He was feeling restless again. Alfred had friends help him write letters to Father Provençal, his good friend back in Saint-Césaire. He told Father Provençal that even in the United

States he hadn't been able to find a job he could work at. He also told the priest how much his devotion to Saint Joseph was growing. Father Provençal answered him. "Come home, Alfred. Come back home."

3

HOME AT LAST

Alfred returned to Canada in 1867. After staying with some relatives in a town close to the United States border, he settled down near Saint-Césaire. Father Provençal heartily welcomed him. "Let's talk about your plans for the future, your hopes and dreams," the kind priest invited. Father could see that his friend was very discouraged. "Have you ever thought of entering the religious life, Alfred?" he questioned.

The young man's eyebrows shot up in surprise. "You know that I can't read or write, Father," he answered sadly. "How could I ever hope to be accepted?"

"It doesn't matter, Alfred," the priest replied. "It's not that you *can't* learn. You've just never had the opportunity. I'm sure you would learn to read and write with the brothers." Father Provençal smiled as he continued. "The life of a brother is different from that of a priest. The main requirement is that you know how to pray! Not all of the brothers are teachers. Some of our brothers dedicate themselves to manual work, just like their patron, Saint Joseph, did."

Alfred's eyes grew bright at the mention of Saint Joseph. His heart pounded. Maybe this was the answer to all his searching. Maybe God wanted him to be a brother.

Father Provençal continued, "Have you seen the boarding school across the street from the rectory? It's run by the Congregation of Holy Cross. The Congregation is made up of priests, brothers, and sisters. The brothers here teach in the school, but, as I explained, not every brother of the Congregation is a teacher."

"I'll have to pray and think about this, Father," Alfred responded. "There's just so much to consider."

The Congregation of Holy Cross had an interesting history. Its founder, Father Basil Moreau, originally saw the need for priests who would serve the poor in the city of Le Mans, France. He organized a group of priests for this work. They became known as the Auxiliary Priests of Le Mans. About twenty years earlier, another French priest named Father Jacques Dujarie, had founded a congregation of religious brothers to instruct young Catholics in their faith. When Father Dujarie's health worsened and he could no longer lead the brothers, the bishop of Le Mans placed them under the direction of Father Moreau. In 1840, the Auxiliary Priests merged with a community of religious brothers called the Brothers of Saint Joseph. With Father Moreau as their superior, they formed the new Congregation of Holy Cross. In 1841, Father Moreau also added a society of sisters to his religious family. (Pope Benedict XVI beatified Father Basil Moreau on September 15, 2007.)

Not long after his talk with Father Provençal, Alfred got up enough courage to visit the Brothers of Holy Cross. Father Provençal had already spoken to them about Alfred. For their part, the religious weren't too enthusiastic about a prospective postulant who couldn't read or write and was always sick besides!

Alfred spent almost the entire day before the meeting in prayer. He asked Saint Joseph to show him God's will. The important day came. Alfred sat opposite two of the Holy Cross brothers in a bare parlor. He silently studied their habit. The black robe resembled a priest's cassock. It was topped with a Roman collar. A long woolen cincture, a kind of rope edged with tassels, served as a belt. The habit was completed by a plain wooden cross and a medal of Saint Joseph. Alfred shifted nervously in his chair. The brothers kindly answered his questions. They told him about their school. But that was all. They didn't encourage him to apply for admission. Finally, one of them asked, "Why do you want to enter our congregation, Alfred? Are you certain that you have a vocation to religious life?"

The young man's eyes were on fire. He leaned forward. "I know that I'm uneducated and won't be able to teach as you do. But even though my health is not good, I can work. And I'm willing to work—to do any kind of odd jobs. Your congregation is devoted to Saint Joseph, and that's why I want to be part of it. Somehow, I just know that Saint Joseph wants me to work for him."

The brothers eyed each other in silent surprise. In spite of their doubts, they found themselves promising Alfred that they would speak to their superiors about him and recommend that he be accepted as a postulant!

On November 22, 1870, twenty-five-year-old Alfred Bessette arrived on the doorstep of Notre Dame College in Montreal, Canada. Notre Dame also served as the novitiate of the Congregation of Holy Cross. A note to the superior of the school had preceded Alfred there. It was from Father Provençal. One sentence seemed to jump off the page: "I'm sending you a saint!"

4

AN ACT OF DARING

Alfred felt as if he had stepped into a whole new world. And it was one in which he finally felt completely at home. The long gray building on the slopes of Mount Royal seemed like a slice of heaven to the new postulant. "Thank you for bringing me here, Lord," Alfred whispered over and over. "Thank you, too, Saint Joseph."

In his first weeks, the newcomer got used to the hours of prayer and work. It wasn't always easy to obey and follow a strict schedule. After all, Alfred had been living on his own for ten years. But he smiled as he washed dishes, mended clothes, and scrubbed floors.

That December, just a month after his entrance into the community, Alfred was accepted as a novice. He received the habit of the Brothers of Holy Cross. A sense of peace and joy enfolded him as he knelt in the chapel ablaze with candles and bright Christmas flowers. As the presiding priest placed the folded black robe into his outstretched hands, he heard the words,

"Alfred Bessette, from now on your name will be Brother André." A tingle of excitement raced through his body. How wonderful! He had received the name of his friend and mentor Father André Provençal. It was a very happy day for Brother André. But a long struggle still lay ahead . . .

As a novice, André's work assignments included taking care of the community's linen, helping in the infirmary, and keeping the corridors orderly and clean. André put his whole heart into every duty. A few months into his novitiate, however, talk began to circulate that the provincial council was not going to allow Brother André to make his vows. His superiors were afraid that his health wouldn't hold out. André was sad and worried. He prayed that he wouldn't be sent away.

"You'd better finish scrubbing the floor, Brother André, the bishop may be coming out into the hall soon," Father Hupier, his spiritual advisor, whispered. André gave the priest a grateful smile. "I'm almost finished, Father," he replied. "I just have this last corner left."

Seventy-two-year-old Bishop Ignace Bourget, the Bishop of Montreal, had come to visit the college. He was a holy and learned man who had a dream for Montreal: he wanted to build a shrine to Saint Joseph where pilgrims could come to pray. Little did he know that the very ordinary young man he was about to meet would be the one to make this dream come true.

Brother André straightened up, put down his scrub brush, and slipped off his damp apron. His eyes were riveted on the door of the guest room. He waited for Father Provincial to emerge from his meeting with the bishop.

The door soon opened, and the provincial superior walked out. André's fingers trembled as he made the Sign of the Cross. He murmured a quick prayer to Saint Joseph. It was now or never! He darted across the hall and knocked hastily at the door of the bishop's room.

"Come in," came the response.

André rushed in and fell to his knees.

"What is it, my son?" the kindly bishop inquired with a look of surprise.

Brother André kissed Bishop Bourget's ring then began to explain. Everything he wanted to say came out in one breath. "Your

"Your Excellency, I'm afraid I won't be allowed to make my vows."

Excellency, I'm afraid that I won't be allowed to make my vows as a brother," he stammered. "My superiors tell me that I don't have the strength for the work. Please, Your Excellency, I want to serve God. I know that he'll give me the health I need to fulfill my duties."

Brother André paused. His clear dark eyes met those of the bishop. André's voice softened to a plea: "My life is here, Your Excellency. Must I leave the place I love so much?"

"Don't be afraid," the bishop answered. "You will be permitted to make your vows."

"Thank you, Your Excellency! Oh, thank you!" André exclaimed, quickly rising to his feet. Back in the hall, he breathed a sigh of relief. *I owe this favor to you, Lord,* he silently prayed, *and to Saint Joseph.*

Father Guy, the novice master, also pleaded Brother André's cause before the Holy Cross Provincial Council.

"But Father, be reasonable," one of the Council members interjected. "If this novice gets sick and isn't able to work, he'll become a burden to the congregation."

"If this young man becomes unable to work," Father Guy argued, "he'll still be able to pray. And that's what's most important. I can assure you that this young brother can teach us all to pray."

Brother André made his first vows of poverty, chastity, and obedience on August 22, 1872 in the Congregation of Holy Cross. He would make his final vows on February 2, 1874.

After Brother André became an official member of the Congregation of Holy Cross through his taking of vows, he received a new assignment. But no one could have imagined what was about to happen . . .

5

A Shrine Is Born

"Brother André, your main duty from now on will be to serve as porter, answering the front door of the school and greeting our guests," his superior explained. Later on, André loved to joke, "At the end of my novitiate, my superiors showed me the door, and I worked there for forty years!"

It was true. For forty years, the humble brother answered the door and did many other odd jobs around Notre Dame College, a school attended by over 200 boys between the ages of seven and twelve. After having given quick haircuts to a few of the boys, André developed a reputation as the school barber. He charged the grand total of five cents a haircut! As he cut their hair, André always talked to the boys about praying to Saint Joseph. And he carefully saved the nickels he received for a secret project he had in mind.

Because he had to be available to answer the door, Brother André slept in a small room about ten feet long by six feet wide. (Luckily, he was a tiny person himself. He was only five feet tall.) One small window lit the dim room. A wardrobe, a bench, a chair, and a small desk made up the room's sparse furnishings. A thinly padded couch was the only bed.

Besides answering the door, André was in charge of the mail, running errands in town, picking up the students' laundry from their parents' homes (for which he used a horse and buggy), and keeping the front parlor and surrounding corridors tidy. In the evenings, he made cinctures, the special belts the brothers wore on their habits. He also did whatever chores needed to be finished around the house.

In the middle of all this busyness, Brother André prayed. He attended morning Mass kneeling by the door at the back of the chapel in case the doorbell rang. He couldn't join the other brothers for some of the other daily prayers because he had to remain at his post at the front door. But that didn't matter to Brother André. He could pray anywhere. And he did! The crucifix on the bare wall of his room and the chipped little statue of Saint Joseph on his desk helped to remind him of Jesus and the Guardian of the Holy Family. André was always so happy when a brother would offer to take his place at the door so that he could slip away to the chapel. The trouble was that once Brother André got there, he fell into such a deep conversation with God that he lost all track of time. "But Brother, you've been praying for two hours already," his exasperated substitute once told him. "You promised me that you'd only be gone for fifteen minutes. I can't stay at the door any longer. I have a class to teach!"

André also spent many nights praying in the chapel after everyone else had gone to sleep. Another brother decided to put a stop to this. One night, he locked the chapel door. Then he hid nearby waiting to see what André would do. When André arrived, he put his hand on the locked door and it simply opened!

"Brother André got into the chapel through a locked door last night," the spy reported at breakfast the next morning. "Sure," a brother chuckled, "and you were the only witness, right? You'd better get some extra sleep tonight before *you* have more hallucinations!"

All during this time, Brother André continued to suffer from his stomach problems. Most of the time his "meal" consisted of a crust of bread dipped in some milk and water. He hurriedly ate by himself because his job answering the door didn't allow him to have meals at the usual hours.

Some of the brothers found André a bit odd. For example, the brother in charge of the community's bookkeeping always knew when Brother André had been in to tidy up the accounting office. For some strange reason, a little statue of Saint Joseph would always be turned to face out the window that overlooked Mount Royal. Finally, the curious brother could stand it no longer. "Why in the world do you keep turning Saint Joseph toward the window?" he burst out one day when he caught Brother André with the statue in his hand.

"Because he wants to be honored on the mountain," André replied with a smile. "I turn him toward it so that he can enjoy the view."

As his answer showed, Brother André was a simple man. The students and their parents found it easy to speak to him. They loved and admired him for his faith, his common sense, and especially for his friendliness. In fact, it was becoming difficult for Brother André to find a few moments alone. The children of Notre Dame were always running after him. They wanted to watch him pray, or see what kind of work he was doing, or get their hair cut. He never became impatient with the boys. He enjoyed their company and always told them stories about Saint Joseph. With his visitors, Brother André also prayed to Saint Joseph. Unusual things began to happen. Soon the word began to spread, first among the students' parents and then among the townspeople. "Brother André can work miracles!"

"Brother André! Brother André!" ten-year-old Henri called after him one spring day. "I saw you climbing the mountain yesterday. Where were you going all by yourself?"

André ruffled the boy's thick hair and smiled. "I went up the mountain where it's nice and quiet to pray to Saint Joseph. Would you like to come with me if your mother gives you permission?"

"Sure!" the boy excitedly answered.

"Well run home and ask her, and meet me here after supper."

Later that day, Brother André and Henri climbed a path to a large clearing on Mount Royal. A few of the older boys followed along. When they reached the top, they stood in silence for a few moments. The Canadian landscape was breathtaking. Dark green pines, white birches, and sturdy maple trees blanketed the mountainside. From their vantage point, the Saint Lawrence River seemed to be dancing its way into Lake Saint Louis. In the distance, bare purple mountains stood like sentinels crowned with white snow. Lifting their peaks to the sky, they wrapped themselves in wisps of clouds.

No wonder Brother André comes up here, Henri thought. *It's beautiful!*

"I'm going to tell you my dream, Henri," Brother André confided with a twinkle in his eye. "I've buried a medal of Saint Joseph by this tree. I come here every day to pray that my congregation will be able to purchase this land. Saint Joseph needs it for the shrine he wants. Let's kneel now and say a prayer."

Brother André led a prayer to Saint Joseph, the patron of Canada and of the Catholic Church. The boys answered, "Amen." As they stood to leave, André took one more look around. "We *will* buy this land some day, Henri. Wait and see. Just wait and see!"

6

THE MIRACLES BEGIN

A feverish young boy tossed and turned in the infirmary bed. The damp towel on his forehead was already drying up. Doctor Joseph Charette looked up at the brother in charge. "I can't seem to get his temperature down. It's been high for several days now. He must stay in bed until the fever breaks. Keep the cool towels on him. Let's see if that helps."

"Thank you, Doctor," the brother replied. "I will. Let me see you to the door."

Not long after the doctor had left, the attending brother returned with fresh towels. Brother André quietly entered the room.

Pausing at the side of the feverish student, he shook his head. "So, I hear you're being lazy today," he said with a smile. "What are you doing in bed? You're not sick!"

"But I am, Brother," the boy protested. "Even Dr. Charette said I am. He's the one who told me to stay in bed. I feel so hot . . ."

"You're not sick!" André insisted. "You should be out playing with your friends."

"Now get out of that bed ... you're not sick!"

"Now get out of that bed, dress up, and go outside. You'll be in time for recess." And with that, Brother André was gone.

The boy, already beginning to feel much better, jumped out of bed and hurriedly changed his clothes. He left the infirmary and was soon happily playing in the school-yard.

A little while later an angry rapping on the front door interrupted Brother André's work. André answered the door to find himself face to face with a very irritated Doctor Charette. The doctor, a sincere Catholic, served as the school physician besides running a large medical practice in Montreal.

"Who do you think you are, telling that student to do just the opposite of what I had ordered?" the doctor bellowed. "That boy has a severe fever . . . it could even be small-pox. He shouldn't be outside—especially with other children!"

"The boy has no fever," Brother André calmly replied.

"What do you mean? I examined him myself. His fever is dangerously high!"

"Examine him one more time, Doctor," André quietly said. "You will find that he is perfectly well."

"I'll do just that!" retorted the doctor. "Bring him here immediately."

Doctor Charette took the student's temperature again, and it was normal. At day's end, the doctor left the school muttering, "I don't understand. I've taken his temperature three different times and there isn't even a trace of fever. I've never seen such a high fever simply disappear . . ."

Not long after the young boy got well, an epidemic of smallpox broke out at Saint–Laurent College, another school run by the Congregation of Holy Cross. The dread disease struck down students and religious alike. Some even died. Father Beaudet, the superior at Saint-Laurent, asked for volunteers to help the sick who were being isolated from the rest of the community. Brother André answered the call even though his own health was not strong. It's said that when he arrived at Saint-Laurent, he went straight to the chapel and fell on his knees, begging God through the intercession of Saint Joseph to stop the spread of the disease. After this prayer, all those who were ill soon recuperated, and no new cases of smallpox were reported.

Rumors were soon circulating about another miraculous cure involving Brother

André in November of 1884. A woman, so crippled by rheumatism that she couldn't walk, was brought by her friends to see André. When she arrived, Brother André was on his knees scrubbing the floor of the school's parlor.

"There he is," the brother who opened the door, pointed out. "Brother André, this woman suffers from severe rheumatism. She insisted on being brought to you."

"Let her walk," André said quietly as he continued to scrub the floor.

"Tell him to pay attention!" the woman exclaimed. "I want to be able to walk again. I've come a long way to see him and he's . . . he's just ignoring me!"

"André," pleaded the brother, "could you at least say something to her?"

Brother André looked up long enough to tell the irritated woman, "You're not crippled any more. You can return home now." Then he calmly continued his work.

The invalid scowled. Her body still ached, and this supposed "miracle man" didn't even seem to care. But suddenly, she realized what André had just said.

Turning to the friends who were supporting her, she said, "Please, let me go. I think I can walk." In an instant she felt her legs grow straight and strong. Her knotted hands grew smooth and pliable again. All her pain disappeared.

"Brother André, I'm well!" the woman cried. "I'm cured!"

"Don't thank me," he replied with a smile. "Thank Saint Joseph. Go now and say a prayer to him in the chapel."

André always gave the credit for any cures to Saint Joseph. "Pray to Saint Joseph and I'll pray, too," was his advice to each sick person who came to see him. "I'm nothing . . . just a tool in God's hands, a humble instrument for Saint Joseph to use. Anyone who thinks that I can work miracles is silly! It is God and Saint Joseph who heal people, not I. Here is a good way to pray to Saint Joseph. Tell him, 'What would you do if you were in my place, Saint Joseph? What would you want to be done for you? Well, ask God for this blessing on my behalf.'"

News of these miracles, which began when Brother André was about thirty years old, spread like wildfire in the surrounding towns and villages. And, just as quickly, crowds of the sick began to arrive. Soon throngs of people were ringing the school's doorbell clamoring to see Brother André.

André prayed to Saint Joseph with each one. To every sick person he gave a medal of the saint. He would rub a medal, and sometimes olive oil taken from a lamp that burned in front of the statue of Saint Joseph, over the problem area of a sick person's body. For example, if someone had an injured leg, he'd rub it with the Saint Joseph medal and oil as he prayed.

More and more people went away cured. "I don't cure. It's Saint Joseph who does!" Brother André repeatedly insisted. Still, the superior of the college was annoyed. So was Doctor Charette. "Brother André is a quack," he protested. "He should stop all this nonsense immediately!"

7

TROUBLE

To make matters worse, a group of the students' parents became upset about Brother André's healing ministry. They were worried that their children would be infected by some of the sick who suffered from contagious diseases. "You either stop these sick persons from visiting Brother André or we'll send our children to another school!" they threatened.

Things were getting out of hand. So the superior asked Brother André to stop having the sick visit him at the school. As a kind of compromise, André began to meet visitors in the trolley station acrosss the street. "You can pray with the sick over there," his superior told him. Brother André obeyed. And the people continued to come, even in bad weather.

Meanwhile, Doctor Charette never let a chance go by to call Brother André names, or tell people what a fake he was. Then one day his wife got a serious nosebleed. The doctor couldn't stop it. He called in some colleagues, but they couldn't control the bleeding either.

His wife begged him, "Joseph, if you really love me, send for Brother André."

"What!" he cried. "Bring that quack into this house? Never!"

"Then I will die," his wife said simply. "I'm losing too much blood. I'm feeling weaker and weaker by the minute . . ."

Doctor Charette was shaken when he heard these words. Swallowing his pride, he quietly left the house and rushed to get Brother André. André kindly agreed to go with the doctor. On their way back to the house, he told him, "Don't worry. Your wife will not die." As soon as Brother André stepped into Mrs. Charette's room, her bleeding stopped. She never had the problem again. From that day on, Doctor Charette became one of Brother André closest friends and supporters.

At certain times, even diocesan authorities became suspicious of Brother André. They couldn't see how rubbing Saint Joseph's oil or a medal on the sick and encouraging them to pray a novena to the saint could result in so many cures.

To those who questioned his "methods," Brother André matter-of-factly replied, "God gave us our senses. We need to see, and touch, and feel. So, I tell the sick to make a novena and rub themselves with the medal and the oil of Saint Joseph. It's a way of showing confidence in Saint Joseph's power of intercession with God."

Sometimes people accused the humble brother of believing in magic. But Brother André insisted that the medal was a sign of faith. Whenever a person had some problem he would say, "Take a medal of Saint Joseph with you, and hold it in your hand while you pray. You'll see. Saint Joseph will help you."

At one point, the Board of Health was even drawn into the uproar over Brother André and his work with the sick. Fortunately, they investigated and reported that André's actions were "harmless."

When Archbishop Paul Bruchesi heard about the complaints against Brother André, he called in the Provincial Superior of the Holy Cross community. "Will Brother André stop this work if you order him to?" the archbishop asked.

"Of course, Your Excellency. He's very obedient." the provincial responded.

"Good. Then leave him alone," said the archbishop. "If the work is from God, it will continue. If not, it will disappear by itself."

8

Saint Joseph Gets His Wish

"Six years have passed since I buried a medal of Saint Joseph on Mount Royal," Brother André confided to a student one day. "And every day I've gone up that mountain to pray that part of the land would belong to my Congregation of Holy Cross. Now it does! Saint Joseph helped us to buy it!"

And so he did. In 1896, the Congregation of Holy Cross purchased about twenty-five acres of the mountain that bordered their college. André and the brothers immediately got to work. They widened the path that André had always used, giving it the name "Saint Joseph's Boulevard." Halfway up the mountain they cleared an open space beneath the trees. They even carved out steps in the rocks at the steepest points of the climb. Once the area was cleared, Brother André, happily carrying a statue of Saint Joseph holding the Christ Child, led a little procession up the mountain. He placed the statue in an opening in a rock. André dreamed of constructing a *real* chapel for Saint Joseph someday.

The brothers used the lower part of this ground to grow vegetables. But from the top of Mount Royal, visitors had a magnificent view of the landscape below. A year later, Brother André put a little dish beside the statue of Saint Joseph, which he had set up on the mountain. Its purpose was to hold the coins which visitors might wish to leave there in honor of the saint. Meanwhile, Brother André, who was continuing to receive the sick, encouraged them to climb the mountain to enjoy the beautiful view and pray at the simple shrine. Every evening when he went up the mountain to pray, André would also count the few cents in the dish. "More donations for Saint Joseph!" he'd happily exclaim.

Brother André had received permission from his superior to save the "dish money" for a future project. Once in a while, he also added some of the nickels he earned cutting hair. After six years, André had collected 200 dollars, a substantial amount at the time. But how would he convince his superior to build a chapel on the mountain? That's where the Lord took over . . .

One day, Brother André got sick. He was sent to the infirmary. The other patient in his room just happened to be his superior, Father Lecavalier. Since neither one was seriously ill, they had plenty of time to talk. This gave Brother André a chance to speak about his dream of building a chapel in honor of Saint Joseph. Father Lecavalier also had great devotion to Saint Joseph. "But where will we get the money, André?" he asked.

"Oh, I've collected 200 dollars so far—if you'll give me permission to use it, Father. And Brother Abundius is a wonderful carpenter. It will be a very small chapel, Father, very small. It won't even have windows." By the time the two left the infirmary, Brother André had the permission he needed to get started on the chapel!

While certain people continued to gossip and distrust Brother André's healing prayers, the sick continued to flock to his door. One evening, a young man supported by the strong arm of a friend, appeared at the college asking for Brother André. "We'll have to go across the street," André started to explain. "I'm not allowed to have visitors at the school." There was something about this young man that looked strangely familiar. "Henri!" André suddenly shouted. "You're little Henri all grown up. You were the first one to come and pray with me on the mountain."

Henri smiled. "I knew he'd remember me," he told his companion.

"What's wrong, Henri?" Brother André asked with concern. "You look so pale."

"I had an accident at work. My left leg is full of infection and the doctor wants to amputate it. I know you can cure me."

"Not me, Henri," said André shaking his head. "But Saint Joseph can ask God for this favor if you have faith."

"I do!" Henri answered.

"I know you do. Now you're going to stay right here with me. Your friend can return home. Come, I'll show you a bed you can rest in."

Later that evening when Brother André returned to his room after finishing his chores, he examined Henri's leg. It was black and swollen. André sat by the bed and rubbed Henri's leg first with a medal of Saint Joseph and then with olive oil from a lamp that burned before the saint's statue. He continued this for a long time, praying all the while. After a few hours, the leg was so healthy that Henri was able to walk back home over the slippery, snow-covered village roads!

André smiled. What did it matter what some people thought of him. Saint Joseph was using him to do good. That was the important thing.

9

A Dream Takes Shape

Brother André was no carpenter. Luckily, his friend Brother Abundius was. By the end of the summer of 1904, the two had used André's "dish money" to buy lumber for their special project. The mountain chapel they were going to build, dedicated to Saint Joseph, would be small—just eighteen feet long and fifteen feet wide. Before long, Mount Royal echoed with the sounds of hammer and saw. André thought of every detail.

"Where will the windows go, Brother André?" asked one of the lay volunteers who faithfully came to help.

"Well, windows are expensive," André answered slowly. "We can let in just as much light if we insert a pane of glass in the roof."

"What a good idea!"

Some workers needed to be hired to complete the project, but André's original 200 dollars had run out. In his strong faith, Brother André simply placed the famous dish beside the front door of the new chapel.

There always seemed to be just enough money in it to pay the workers!

When the last nail had been hammered, Brother André stood back to survey the chapel. "What do you think, Abundius? Isn't it fine? It's small, but it's a beginning."

"I'm sure Saint Joseph is pleased," Brother Abundius smiled.

"Now we must continue to ask him to provide a bigger and better chapel in the future," Brother André mused. "Yes, a bigger and better one! But we're not done here yet. We have to widen the path into a road. It's not large enough for all the pilgrims who'll be coming."

"Pilgrims?" Brother Abundius asked in surprise.

"Of course," André replied. "Saint Joseph wants to be honored here by many pilgrims."

"If you say so," Abundius answered, shaking his head.

A few days later, the school's doorbell rang. Brother André, now sixty years old, rushed to answer it. There stood a tall, gaunt man with calloused hands. He was Calixte Richard, the brother of one of the students.

"Are you Brother André?" Calixte asked.

André raised his eyebrows. A smile lit his face. Clasping his hands together he exclaimed, "Yes, I am! And you're just the man I'm looking for! Could you come and work for me tomorrow morning?"

"Work for you?" Calixte repeated in amazement. "Brother, I have a stomach tumor. I can barely eat. I haven't been able to work for three years. I used to be employed at the stone quarry . . ."

"Wonderful!" Brother André broke in. "We need you to help us make a road up to the chapel. Come and have breakfast with me in the morning. Then we'll see what can be done."

The astonished man agreed to come back the next morning. Then, shaking his head, he turned and began his walk home. *Maybe Brother didn't understand what I said*, he thought. *I hope I won't disappoint him.*

The following morning, Calixte, true to his word, returned to the monastery. He sat down with Brother André to a table laden with steaming eggs and sausages, fresh fruit, and a strong pot of coffee with cream and sugar. "Help yourself," said Brother André as he filled the man's plate. "Eat well. You'll work hard today." All the while, André kept telling him that Saint Joseph would cure him permanently if he kept his part of the bargain.

"Brother André, I haven't worked in years. I'm very weak," the man explained again. Obviously, Brother André wasn't paying attention to his protests. Since Calixte had no stomach pains and actually felt hungry, he began to eat . . . slowly at first, then faster. Brother André filled his plate until he had finished the entire breakfast right down to the last drop of coffee!

Brother André looked on with delight. Giving a squeeze to Calixte's shoulder, he urged, "To work, now! There's much to be done!"

"All right, Brother. I'm ready. I feel so much better. I haven't felt like this in ages."

Calixte worked for Brother André for several months until the road was complete. All symptoms of his cancer had disappeared.

10

BIGGER AND BETTER

The mountain chapel was dedicated by Monsignor Racicot on October 19, 1904. "It will be called Saint Joseph's Oratory," said Brother André proudly. That day, a statue of the saint was blessed in the Notre Dame College Chapel. It was carried up Mount Royal in procession and placed on the little white altar built by Brother Abundius. Brother André himself decorated the altar with flowers. Then Holy Mass was celebrated.

But André's great happiness didn't last long. The tiny chapel soon had to be closed temporarily because of weather conditions. It had no heating system, and pilgrims couldn't pray there during the long and harsh Canadian winters.

When the Oratory reopened in the spring, Brother André loved to make the Stations of the Cross there in the evenings. Some of the volunteers who had helped build the Oratory began to accompany him. André moved reverently from station to station. He added his own spontaneous prayers to those he read aloud from a prayer book. More than one person who attended these prayers testified to seeing the humble brother "surrounded by a bright light" in the midst of the dark little chapel. Later on, André invited some of his friends to make Holy Hours at the Oratory of Saint Joseph. As more and more people witnessed André pray, they began to recognize his true holiness.

Soon enough, however, there were loud grumblings about the Oratory. When too many visitors came in the rain or other bad weather, they had to stand outside. "There's just not enough room for everyone," one man complained. "My wife and I ended up in the pouring rain during Mass. We got soaked to the skin!"

In 1908, four years after the original chapel had been built, Brother André and his provincial superior, Father Dion, visited Archbishop Paul Bruchesi to ask his permission to enlarge it.

"Do you have a medal of Saint Joseph to take with you?" André anxiously asked his superior.

"No," Father Dion replied, slipping into his overcoat.

"Here . . . take this one," Brother André offered. "Hold it tightly in your hand while you're talking to the archbishop about the plans for the addition. Saint Joseph will help us."

Archbishop Bruchesi was happy to give his permission to enlarge the chapel—as long as the Holy Cross Congregation could raise the needed funds. Brother André had faith that Saint Joseph would do his part by sending the necessary donations.

André had good news for his faithful team of volunteers and workmen a few days later. "We're going to add a roof supported by posts to the Oratory," he explained. "Then we'll wall up the whole area so that it forms a new section of the building. From now on, the Oratory will also be heated during the winter. This will make things much easier for the pilgrims who come to pray to Saint Joseph. They'll be able to visit in all kinds of weather!"

Brother André's dedicated group of friends organized themselves to collect money for the project. By that November, the renovations were complete. The following year another small building was constructed. It housed a restaurant and rest area for pilgrims and a small bedroom and office space for Brother André. Once this building was ready, Brother André received a new assignment. He left his post at the front door of the college to become the official guardian of the Oratory of Saint Joseph! He was thrilled with his new work.

But there was one problem. André still hadn't found a permanent chaplain for the chapel on the mountain. He continued to encourage all the sick persons who visited him to pray at Saint Joseph's Oratory. He also advised many of them to go to confession. Since the little chapel was without a priest, however, Brother André couldn't be sure that they would really receive the sacrament later on. The Holy Cross priests had many responsibilities in the parishes of the Montreal area, so it was difficult to find a priest to care for the needs of the pilgrims. "Saint Joseph will provide," André said simply to one of the brothers. "He always does."

11

THE BLIND SHALL SEE

Brother André soon decided to give Saint Joseph a nudge in the right direction. He scheduled an appointment with his provincial superior, back at Notre Dame College.

"Brother André!" the priest said warmly, extending his arms to welcome him. "It's good to see you. How's everything going at the Oratory?"

"We're missing something very important, Father," André replied as the two sat down at a small table.

Father Dion looked puzzled. "And what might that be?"

"We have no priest to offer daily Mass and hear confessions, Father. Could you assign a full-time chaplain to the Oratory?"

Father Dion ran his hand through his thinning hair. He hadn't expected such a request. "I wish I could, André," he said shaking his head. "But I have none to spare."

André wasn't ready to give up. "What about Father Adolphe Clement?" he ventured.

Father Dion looked startled. "Adolphe is young and strong, but he's going blind. That's why he can't teach anymore. You know that. The doctors tell him his sight will only get worse." Father Dion shook his head sadly. "Right now, he can no longer pray the Divine Office from his breviary. He can still read the Mass prayers from the missal because of the larger print. But he's having a hard time with the daily Scripture readings. What kind of help could he give you?"

"I know all that, Father. But please . . . send him anyway."

"All right, André, all right," the superior sighed.

The next day, a brother from the college led Father Adolphe Clement up the steep road to the Oratory. A cloudless blue sky stretched itself over the mountain. Father Clement saw only a blur. He listened intently to the birds chirping and the pebbles crunching under his feet.

"We're almost there, Father," announced his guide.

Brother André came out of the residence to greet him. Smiling, he took the young priest by the hand. "I've been waiting for you!" he exclaimed. "You'll be a great help to the pilgrims, celebrating Mass every day and hearing confessions."

"You do understand my situation," the priest replied, "I mean, Father Dion has explained everything, right?"

"Yes, Father, I know," André assured him. "Don't worry. I'm making you a promise through Saint Joseph, whom you've come to work for. Tomorrow you will read your breviary again, and you'll begin celebrating daily Mass here at the Oratory."

The next morning before Mass, Father Clement sat by the window. He opened his prayer book. The sunlight fell onto words that were clear and sharp! The excited priest read the prayers with joy. Soon after, Father Clement celebrated his first Mass in the chapel dedicated to Saint Joseph.

In 1910, more construction began to enlarge the Oratory again. A steeple and bell were also added, together with a new attic-like bedroom for Brother André under the chapel's roof. Three thousand pilgrims crowded the mountain to witness the blessing of the new bell. By this time, three Masses a day were being celebrated at the Oratory of Saint Joseph.

Father Clement remained at the Oratory for more than twenty-five years. To the amazement of his eye doctors who kept insisting that he *shouldn't* be able to read because he was *blind*, Father Clement read without any trouble. He wore glasses only during the last few years of his life.

Father Clement became Brother André's "right hand man." He helped to receive and minister to the pilgrims who came to the Oratory. He witnessed many miracles on Mount Royal. One in particular impressed him very much. A man whose feet had been crushed in a work accident came to see Brother André. His feet were in such bad condition that his friends had made wooden boxes to cover them. When Brother André saw him, he began to rub the boxes.

Father Clement thought this was amazing. "What are you doing, Brother?" he asked. "You don't really believe that rubbing the boxes will make his feet grow back, do you?"

André didn't answer. Instead, he prayed and continued to rub the boxes for four days. Then he turned to the friends who had brought the man to the Oratory. "You can take off the boxes now," he said. "I think his feet are doing well." When the boxes were removed, the man's feet were completely healed!

Father Clement admitted, "I thought I knew better than you, Brother André. From now on, I'll respect your methods—even if they are different."

"It's not necessary to be educated or gifted in order to love God and do good," André responded with a smile. "All you have to do is want to love him with your whole heart."

12

MORE MIRACLES

"God lets Saint Joseph work miracles through Brother André!" the people proclaimed. And it was certainly true. In one year alone, 435 cases of healings were reported. As throngs of pilgrims daily climbed the mountain to see André, a monastery was built for the priests and brothers who assisted in welcoming them all.

In 1912, a little magazine called *The Annals of Saint Joseph* was also begun. Within a year, the subscribers grew from 300 to over 4,500. Word of Saint Joseph's great power with God, and of his good friend, Brother André, continued to spread.

Archbishop Bruchesi, who now dreamed of an impressive basilica to Saint Joseph on Mount Royal, considered the Oratory a "mustard seed" that was destined to grow. He blessed the remodeled chapel in the spring of 1912. Looking around at the canes, crutches, eyeglasses, and various braces that had been left at the chapel as testimony of the cures that had taken place, the archbishop said, "Shall I say that miracles have

In one year, 435 cures were reported.

been worked here? If I were to deny it, I'd be contradicted by the medical equipment that surrounds us. It gives witness to every form of suffering . . . But even greater than the physical healings are the spiritual cures that have taken place at the Oratory. I strongly encourage everyone to come here to pray," he told the crowd. "Come often! There's no doubt that Saint Joseph wants to be honored here."

Before he became old and too sick to continue, Brother André received visitors up to seventeen hours a day! Sometimes, because he was tired and not feeling well himself, André would become impatient with people who insisted on being cured. After answering them sharply or hurting their feelings, tears of sorrow would roll down his wrinkled cheeks. His friends then had to try hard to cheer him up. But when he remembered the wonderful things Saint Joseph had done for the people, he'd grow happy again.

One time, a woman suffering from cancer had been scheduled for surgery. She went to see Brother André. "You may go home. You're cured," he simply told her. "Thank Saint Joseph for the blessing he has obtained for you from God."

The woman obeyed and returned home. Her doctor had no faith in Brother André's "miracles." He insisted on going ahead with the operation. But once he began the surgery, he could find no trace of the cancer!

Twenty-six-year-old Emile Laporte worked as a clothes presser in a factory. He used his feet all day to run his industrial ironing board. They had become painfully swollen, and his doctor could offer him no relief. "If this problem continues, Emile, you'll soon lose your ability to stand and walk," he warned.

Emile asked a friend to drive him to Brother André. André spoke kindly to him before examining the man's pitifully swollen feet.

"Now tell me, Emile, what movement do you have to make to operate the presser?"

Without thinking, Emile began to move his legs up and down, up and down. Brother André just shrugged his shoulders and smiled. "Why don't you come back and see me tomorrow?"

When Emile returned the following day, his feet had returned to their normal size. He was completely healed.

Another time, a man carried his little daughter up Mount Royal to see Brother

André. Her thin legs seemed lifeless. The father silently held her before André. Smiling, the brother gently touched her legs and gave her a pat on the head. Then he did something shocking. He motioned with his hand that the man and his daughter should leave! The father felt hot tears welling in his eyes. He blinked them back. *We've come from so far away, and I had such faith that Brother could help us. Why wouldn't God cure my little girl?* He continued walking away, but as he got to the door of André's office, his daughter squirmed in his arms. "Let me go, Daddy!" she cried. "I want to walk *now!*" The worried father looked back at Brother André. "Go ahead," André said. "Put her down." The man obeyed. After grasping her father's hands for her first few tries, the little girl began to walk, very slowly at first and then faster. She practically ran back into her father's outstretched arms as he smiled and wept with joy.

"Go to Saint Joseph," André repeated to all who came. "Beg him to ask God for the graces and favors you need. He won't disappoint you. It's Saint Joseph who cures, not me!"

Once, André was called to the home of a mother who was dying. He got there as quickly as he could. But he was too late. Brother André knelt by the bed of the woman who had apparently just died. He prayed fervently. Then he touched the woman. She suddenly opened her eyes and said, "I'm hungry." André thoughtfully gave her a piece of an orange.

"God is so good!" Brother André used to say. "The cures are not only for those who are healed, but also for the persons who hear about them. It makes their faith stronger."

Not all of the sick persons who came to Brother André were healed. When asked about this, André once explained, "God sometimes grants cures to those whose faith is not very strong in order to strengthen their faith. Those who firmly believe don't need such proof of God's goodness and power."

To those who didn't receive the cure they asked for, Brother André spoke of the sufferings of Jesus. With words of encouragement, he helped them to understand God's great love and care.

Brother André also instructed the pilgrims who didn't obtain a cure to unite their sufferings with those of Jesus. He taught them that the crosses they carried could be joined to the holy cross, and if they offered their struggles to God, he would make good use of them. "Remember that your sufferings help Jesus to lead persons to heaven," Brother André advised. "Accept your sickness now. God will have an eternity to comfort you."

Many persons who weren't sick also came to the Oratory to pour out their troubles to the humble brother. They knew that André was compassionate and wise. Almost everyone who came went away feeling the "miracle" of being more encouraged to face life's problems. "When a person tries his best," Brother André used to say, "he can have confidence in the good God."

13

SPEEDY RECOVERIES

When the sick couldn't come to Brother André, he went to them. After his "office hours" were over, he often visited people in their homes and in the hospitals. Until he was seventy, André made these evening visits on foot or by streetcar. After that, he depended on friends to chauffeur him all over Montreal and beyond. And that was always an adventure. "Faster! Faster!" André would urge. "There are so many people to see and so many things Saint Joseph wants done!"

One of his drivers once chuckled, "Brother André prayed the rosary the whole time we rode around. I know he was praying for the people we would visit, but I hope he was also praying for our safety. I had to be going really fast to keep him happy!"

Of course, driving at high speeds caught them some attention. Most of the Montreal police recognized Brother André and knew about his healing ministry. The familiar wave of his hand gave him safe passage. Except for one time . . .

"Brother André, I think there's a police car behind us," his driver cautioned.

André looked back. "Oh yes, there is," he agreed.

"But I think he wants us to stop," the driver continued. "His lights are flashing."

"Well, let's stop," André matter-of-factly replied. The driver was preparing to receive a ticket when a smiling officer strode up to the car. Thrusting a notepad through the open window he queried, "Brother André, may I please have your autograph?"

The elderly brother obligingly signed his name. It was better than getting a speeding ticket!

Brother André visited the United States every year to spread devotion to Saint Joseph and to collect funds for his beloved Oratory. Once, in need of a rest, he went to stay for a short while with one of his sisters who lived in Woonsocket, Rhode Island. Brother André looked around the house and chose a small bedroom for himself. "Are you sure that's all of your baggage, Alfred?" his sister exclaimed. "There's so little of it!"

"It's everything I need," he replied with a grin.

"Remember, you're supposed to be resting," his sister advised. "No working sixteen or seventeen hours a day here! You really *must* relax."

Brother André smiled. "I can't win," he chuckled as he gave her a grateful hug.

But André's rest was over almost as soon as it began. The local newspaper had leaked the news that he was in Woonsocket. Soon hundreds of people were waiting at the door, with more driving up every minute!

His sister looked out the window in horror. "There's a huge crowd outside, Alfred! We have to do something."

"I'll see them," he said calmly.

"But you're supposed to be on vacation," she moaned.

"I'll rest with the Lord in heaven. Start to line up all the people who wish to see me," he replied. "Saint Joseph will take care of everything."

The crowd of waiting people had snaked its way down two city blocks by the time André's sister opened the front door. Each one had a story to tell, a pain to share, or a favor to ask. "Rub yourself with this medal of Saint Joseph," André advised. "Receive Communion in honor of Saint Joseph," he whispered to another. "Make a novena to Saint Joseph. You'll receive spiritual graces from him," Brother André promised the next visitor.

Many people who stood in line waiting for Brother André late into that evening were cured through the intercession of Saint Joseph. All of them went away strengthened.

Brother André made many trips to the United States during his lifetime. He spread devotion to Saint Joseph, prayed for healing, and encouraged the sick and suffering wherever he went.

Even though huge crowds turned out to see him, André always remained simple and humble. Once, when he was visiting Jersey City, New Jersey, a local parish organized a celebration in his honor. When he got back to Montreal, André happily described the festivities to the priests and brothers of his community without ever realizing that they had all been for *him*. "You should have been there," he said with glowing eyes. "It was really something . . . such beautiful flowers, music, and lights . . . even a procession! It must have been a very important feast day."

14

NEEDED: ONE ROOF

"A larger church is necessary; there's no doubt about it," Archbishop Bruchesi told Brother André's superiors. So many pilgrims had continued to visit Saint Joseph's Oratory that it was again too small. So, in 1915, while World War I was raging in Europe and many beautiful churches and cathedrals were being destroyed by bombs, a great stone church in honor of Saint Joseph was built on Mount Royal. It was called a crypt. This meant that it was a lower level building. The complete plan was to build another church, a great basilica, above and behind it.

When Brother André had a few rare moments to himself, he loved to watch the construction work. *Finally, Saint Joseph will have a real church, not just a chapel,* he thought. *He deserves it!*

It was a happy day for André when the crypt was finished. A nine-foot statue of Saint Joseph, carved from special Italian marble, towered over the main altar. Soon the corridors that led from the entrance doors were covered with crutches, canes, and other medical devices. Persons who had been healed left them behind.

Construction for the huge basilica began in 1924. Of course, it would take millions of dollars to complete the project, and collecting donations took time. The work was stopped and restarted several times. In November of 1936, the unfinished walls of the basilica stood bare and open to the wind and rain. There would be no roof until money could be raised for the project.

A discouraged group of the brothers and priests in charge of the Oratory met that same month. Rain pelted the windows as they discussed how to finance the roof.

"Do you realize how much money it will take to build the roof the architect has in mind?" one priest exclaimed. "Remember, he even wants a dome over it—like the one at Saint Peter's in Rome."

"Can we really afford that?" a brother sighed.

"No," the superior replied. "Still, we can't just leave the building open to the bad weather. Imagine what will happen when the heavy snows come . . ."

"May I make a suggestion?" a timid voice intervened. All eyes turned toward

"Saint Joseph, please find a roof for your basilica!"

ninety-one-year-old Brother André. "We all want to cover the basilica as soon as possible, right?" he continued. "Well, why don't we just place a statue of Saint Joseph in the unfinished church? He'll find himself his own roof. You'll see."

The members of the council smiled at André's simple faith. By this time, they knew him well enough to trust whatever he said. "What are we waiting for?" the superior responded. "Let's bring Saint Joseph into his new home!"

That afternoon, bringing a statue of Saint Joseph with them, the brothers climbed the steep slope to the basilica. They prayed the rosary as they went. Brother André struggled to keep up. He finally had to let the others go on without him. Sitting on a rock, he looked up at the imposing building. *Will I live to see this basilica completed?* he asked himself. *No, but it doesn't matter. My work is almost over. It's almost over.*

Lagging behind, André had been missed. Suddenly, two black-robed brothers came rushing down the hillside to find him. They carried him the rest of the way up.

Brother André placed the small statue of his favorite saint within the huge church. "Saint Joseph, you once provided so well for

Mary and Jesus. Now please find a roof for your basilica!" he prayed aloud.

André was the only one who *wasn't* surprised when Saint Joseph quickly solved the problem. "I knew he'd take care of things," he said with a smile. "He always does." The Congregation of Holy Cross soon received permission to take out a million dollar loan to finance the roof construction. And, if that weren't enough, Brother André set out once again for the United States to collect offerings for the new basilica. It would be his last journey on earth.

15

THE FINAL JOURNEY

Christmas Day in 1936 fell on a Friday. Two brothers smiled as they passed a Christmas crèche in the monastery. Brother André was kneeling before the nativity scene like one of the unmoving statues. "I knew we'd find André here," one whispered. "He just loves thinking about the birth of Jesus."

During the last year of his life, André was only able to meet pilgrims in his office on Wednesday and Sundays. But on the day after Christmas, he drove with a friend to visit a sick person in the nearby town of Saint-Laurent. It was snowing and the roads were slick. As his driver, Joseph Pichette, passed by Our Lady of Hope Hospital, the car suddenly skidded toward the building. "Let's not drive *into* the hospital, Pichette," André joked. "The Sisters would be surprised to see us come in that way!"

"I'm sure that if we would let them know we were coming, they'd open the doors very wide to welcome you," Mr. Pichette replied.

André laughed and then grew thoughtful. "I've noticed how good and caring the Sisters at that hospital are. It's a very peaceful place. You know, Pichette, I think it would be nice to die there."

"What's this talk about dying?" Mr. Pichette countered. "You still have so much good to do!"

After stopping to visit a man who had been healed, the two friends drove back to the Oratory as they had done so many times before. They prayed before the statue of Saint Joseph in the crypt church, and then Mr. Pichette went home. That night, Brother André suffered an attack of gastritis, a painful inflammation of the lining of the stomach. He had always had so many stomach pains that he didn't pay much attention. But by Monday, December 28, there were more problems. André felt sick again. This time, Doctor Lionel Lamy, his physician, thought it might be the flu. "Stay home and rest, Brother," he advised. "I wouldn't go to your office this week."

During the night between December 30 and 31, things got worse. Brother André rang his little bell to call for help. The priest who slept in the next room rushed in. André was trembling with cold. "My right leg is freezing," he managed to say. "It feels just like the North Pole."

On New Year's Eve, Father Cousineau, the superior of the Oratory, and Father Charron, the Holy Cross provincial superior, asked to speak with Doctor Lamy. "We can see that Brother André is not improving," Father Cousineau quietly admitted. "Do you think it would be better to move him to the hospital, Doctor?"

"Definitely," replied Doctor Lamy. "He needs specialized care right now."

They decided to transfer André to Our Lady of Hope, the hospital in the town of Saint-Laurent. As soon as it was dark, Father Cousineau called the ambulance. The superior didn't want people to know that André was leaving the Oratory. He was afraid that if the news got out, crowds would be waiting at the hospital. The brothers wrapped Brother André in so many blankets that only his wrinkled nose could be seen.

André quietly endured his pain all New Year's Day. Father Cousineau stayed by his side.

"Do you suffer very much, Brother?" Father asked him.

"Yes," André replied. "But I thank God for giving me the grace to suffer. I have such a great need of it to make up for my sins. I'm praying and offering God my pains for the Pope and for the end of the war in Spain." (A civil war ravaged Spain from 1936–1939.)

The sister nurses took turns staying beside André's bed day and night. He spoke slowly and carefully. He told stories of the wonderful healings and conversions God had worked through Saint Joseph at the Oratory. One sister bent down and asked softly, "Brother André, why don't you ask Saint Joseph to heal *you*?" André just smiled and sighed. "I can do nothing for myself," he answered. "The Great Almighty is coming soon." Another time he whispered, "Heaven is so beautiful that it's worth all the trouble it takes to prepare for it." He also made a promise: "The construction work will go forward. The basilica of Saint Joseph will be completed."

Not long before midnight on January 4, 1937, Brother André opened his eyes. Many Holy Cross priests and brothers were gathered around his bed. In spite of all his pain, he struggled to speak. "You don't know," he said, "you can never know all the blessings which the good God has given through the Oratory. What misery there is in this world! I was in a position to know about it. But God helped me. I experienced his great power. How good God is! How beautiful! He must be beautiful, because each soul, which is only a reflection of his beauty, is so beautiful!"

Later, the nurse heard him whisper, "Mary, my dear Mother and Mother of my Savior, be merciful to me and help me." Then, "Saint Joseph . . ." Brother André's last words before he fell into a coma were, "Here is the grain . . ." It seems that he was comparing his life and work to the grain of wheat which Jesus talks about in Saint John's Gospel (Jn 12:24). The grain, Jesus says, must die before it can bear much fruit.

On the morning of January 5, Brother André received the Anointing of the Sick (called Extreme Unction at that time). But he never regained consciousness. Now that André was in a coma, the sisters opened the hospital doors to all who wanted to see him. Visitors could no longer tire him. The little brother who had welcomed the sick and suffering for forty years continued to receive them even as he was dying. All day long people filed past André's bed in silence. Some touched rosaries and medals to his wrinkled hands. Others blessed themselves. All whispered prayers for their beloved brother who seemed to be sleeping.

At about 11:30 that night, Brother André took a turn for the worse. With his friends and Holy Cross priests and brothers surrounding him, the prayers for the dying and prayers to Saint Joseph were begun. Father Cousineau removed his own large crucifix. Bending, he gently laid it on André's chest. At 12:50 on the morning of January 6, 1937, the Feast of the Epiphany, the humble brother peacefully made his journey into eternal life. He was ninety-one years old.

16

STILL AT WORK

Fog, rain, and snow descended on Mount Royal in the days after Brother André's death. Even the brutal Canadian winter couldn't stop the people from coming. Over a million people flocked to André's wake and funeral. They came from all over Canada and the United States. Brother André's body was placed in his beloved Oratory. The church remained open day and night to receive the pilgrims. For six days and nights, people came to pay him their last respects. They waited in the freezing weather for four, five, and six hours at a time. Everyone wanted a final glimpse of the little man who had been a brother to all.

The crowds were instructed to enter the Oratory two by two. They walked past the body in single file at the rate of 100 persons a minute in order to give everyone a chance to see Brother André. It was estimated that 75,000 persons passed his coffin each day. Many whispered prayers. Others touched their rosaries and medals to André's body. Newspapers as far away as London and

Paris published the news about the death and funeral of the humble brother

But Brother André was not resting. He was still very much at work doing good for others. Only God can count the number of conversions that took place among those who offered their farewells to the little brother. More physical healings also occurred. On the fourth day of the wake, a woman named Mrs. Ducharme brought her young son Arthur to the Oratory. His arm had been severely crushed in an accident. It was paralyzed. The doctors had given up hope and had told Mrs. Ducharme that the arm would eventually need to be amputated. When it was Arthur's turn to pass by the coffin, he reached out and touched Brother André's body. He was immediately able to move his paralyzed arm! To the amazement of the crowds, he proved that he was cured by picking up and rearranging some chairs. His mother left the Oratory crying tears of joy and gratitude.

The stories of healings and help received through the prayers of Brother André continued to pour in long after he was buried. They still continue today. One very unique event happened in 1942, five years after Brother André's death. Mr. Michel Trudel and his business partner Mr. Joseph Robert owned an appliance store. Because of the shortages caused by World War II, which was going on at that time, they were having trouble ordering appliances to sell. Finally, Mr. Robert had an idea. "Let's put our good friend Brother André on the payroll. Maybe he'll help us." As soon as they started donating Brother André's "salary" to Saint Joseph's Oratory each month, they received more stoves and washing machines than they could sell! Now what could they do?

Mr. Robert came up with another idea. "Let's raise Brother André's salary and make him a salesman," he suggested. After they increased their monthly donation to the Oratory, their business grew by leaps and bounds. Brother André was not going to let himself be outdone in generosity!

The construction of the basilica at Saint Joseph's Oratory continued in 1937 after Brother André's death. The huge dome over the roof was in place later that year. In 1967, the interior decoration of the dome was completed as the building's finishing touch. It is now the largest shrine dedicated to

Saint Joseph in the world, and the largest church in Canada.

Like the good work carried out at Saint Joseph's Oratory, the stories of André's continuing help go on and on. Visitors to the Oratory today can see the many canes, crutches, braces, and wheelchairs that bear silent witness to the stories of miracles still performed through the intercession of Saint Joseph and Brother André. And who can keep track of the still greater spiritual miracles that happen every day?

Brother André Bessette was beatified by Pope John Paul II at Saint Peter's Square in Rome on May 23, 1982. He was canonized by Pope Benedict XVI on October 17, 2010.

Saint André Bessette now continues his work from heaven, where he enjoys the company of the Lord, the Blessed Virgin Mary, and his best friend: Saint Joseph.

PRAYER

Saint Brother André, you had a life full of miracles. How much good you did for others! You show me that faith, kindness, and humility come from loving God, and that simple trust is more important than possessions, accomplishments, or special talents. Your special love for Saint Joseph teaches me that making friends with the saints can help me be closer to God

Saint Brother André, you never gave up on the dream God gave you. No matter what happened, you kept praying and working for what God wanted. Show me how to trust God as you always did. I believe that he has a plan for me, just as he had a plan for you. It's not always easy for me to do what God asks, but that is what I want to do. Help me to spend my life loving God and other people just as you did, in whatever vocation I'm called to.

Please pray for me, Saint André Bessette. Amen.

GLOSSARY

1. **Anointing of the Sick**—the sacrament by which Jesus gives spiritual comfort, strength, and sometimes physical help, to someone who is dangerously ill due to sickness, injury, or old age.

2. **apprentice**—a person who is being taught a specific trade, craft, or art by a professional.

3. **basilica**—a large church of special importance that is patterned after a type of ancient Roman building.

4. **beatification**—the act by which the Pope or his assigned representative declares that a deceased person lived a life of Gospel holiness in a heroic way. This is done after a person's life and holiness have been fully researched. In most cases, a miracle obtained through the holy person's prayers to God is also required. A person who has been beatified is given the title "Blessed."

5. **breviary**—the prayer book containing the Divine Office, also called the Liturgy of the Hours, which is the public and official

common prayer of the Catholic Church. Priests, deacons, and religious brothers and sisters pray the Liturgy of the Hours every day. Many lay people also use this form of prayer, which is based on the Psalms.

6. **canonization**—the act by which the Pope officially declares that someone is a saint in heaven. To canonize someone is to recognize that he or she has lived a life of heroic virtue, is worthy of imitation, and can intercede for others. Like beatification, which it follows, canonization requires a miracle resulting from the holy person's prayers to God.

7. **chaplain**—a priest who ministers to a certain group of people.

8. **chastity, vow of**—by this vow, religious priests, brothers, or sisters freely give up the right to marry, and the privileges and responsibilities that come with being married, in order to dedicate themselves completely to God and the Church.

9. **congregation (religious)**—a community of men or women who live together and make vows of chastity, poverty, and obedience to God. The members of such a congregation are called "religious". They

share a life of prayer and carry out special works of service for the good of God's people.

10. **Epiphany**—"to show" in Greek. The Feast of Epiphany celebrates the first "showing" of the birth of Jesus to non-Jews, the Wise Men who came from the East in search of the Christ Child. This feast is traditionally celebrated on January 6. (Today in the dioceses of the United States, it has been moved to the Sunday between January 2 and January 8.)

11. **habit**—the clothing that identifies a priest, brother, or sister as a member of a religious congregation.

12. **humble**—lowly or meek; the opposite of being proud. A humble person practices the virtue of humility, which makes us realize that everything good in us is a gift of God.

13. **infirmary**—a place where the sick are cared for.

14. **intercession**—a type of prayer in which we ask God's help for a special favor. Jesus intercedes for us to God the Father. We can also pray to God through the intercession of Mary and the other saints.

15. **lay person**—term that usually refers to any member of the Catholic Church who is not a priest, deacon, religious brother, or sister.

16. **midwife**—a person who is trained to help women deliver a baby.

17. **miracle**—a wonderful happening which goes beyond the powers of nature and is produced by God to teach us some truth or to testify to the holiness of a person.

18. **monastery**—the residence of members of a male religious congregation. It can also refer to the place where monks or nuns live, dedicating themselves to a life of prayer.

19. **novena**—nine days of prayer. This custom recalls the time that Mary and the first disciples of Jesus spent praying together between the ascension of Jesus into heaven and the coming of the Holy Spirit on Pentecost.

20. **novice**—a person in the period of training that comes after postulancy and before making vows in religious life.

21. **novice master**—the priest or brother who teaches and guides new members who

are preparing to make their vows in a male religious congregation.

22. **novitiate**—a time in which novices learn about the spirit of their religious congregation through prayer, study, and participation in the community's life and mission. They prepare to make the vows through which they will totally offer their lives to Jesus. The building in which this training takes place is also called the novitiate.

23. **obedience, vow of**—by this vow, a religious promises to obey God's will as it comes through the directives of his or her superiors.

24. **oratory**—a building other than a parish church that is set aside for prayer and the celebration of Mass.

25. **pilgrims**—persons who travel to a holy place to pray and feel closer to God. The journey they make is called a pilgrimage.

26. **postulant**—a person taking his or her first steps in religious life; a candidate. The period of time during which a young man or woman remains a postulant is called postulancy. Postulants ask to be admitted to

the community after they have learned what religious life will involve.

27. **poverty, vow of**—by this vow a religious promises to live a simple life and gives up personal ownership of money and things in imitation of Jesus.

28. **procession**—a religious event in which people walk together from one place to another in order to publicly honor God, the Blessed Virgin, or the saints. Processions may be held indoors or outdoors and usually take place at churches or shrines.

29. **rheumatism**—a disease marked by a painful stiffness of the joints and muscles.

30. **Rosary**—a formal prayer based on the Scriptures in which we think about important events in the lives of Jesus and Mary. The Rosary is made up of Our Father's, Hail Mary's, and Glory's that we pray while using a circle of beads also called a rosary or rosary beads.

31. **shrine**—a holy place. A shrine is usually a place to which people go on pilgrimage to pray and to show their devotion to God, Mary, or one of the saints.

32. **superior, religious** (also *"provincial superior"*)—the person who has authority in a religious community. The superior's authority is described in the rules of the religious congregation and in the laws of the Church. The provincial superior has authority over all the communities of his or her congregation within a certain territory. The provincial superior receives advice and help from the religious who serve on the provincial council.

33. **vocation**—a call from God to love and serve him in a particular state of life. A person may have a vocation to marriage, priesthood, the religious life, or the single life. Everyone has a vocation to be holy.

34. **vow**—a solemn promise freely made to God. Religious priests, brothers, and sisters usually make vows of poverty, chastity, and obedience. The act of making the vows is called "profession".

Who are the Daughters of St. Paul?

We are Catholic sisters. Our mission is to be like Saint Paul and tell everyone about Jesus! There are so many ways for people to communicate with each other. We want to use all of them so everyone will know how much God loves us. We do this by printing books (you're holding one!), making radio shows, singing, helping people at our bookstores, using the Internet, and in many other ways.

Visit our Web site at www.pauline.org

BOOKS & MEDIA

The Daughters of St. Paul operate book and media centers at the following addresses. Visit, call or write the one nearest you today, or find us on the World Wide Web, www.pauline.org

CALIFORNIA
3908 Sepulveda Blvd, Culver City, CA 90230   310-397-8676
2640 Broadway Street, Redwood City, CA 94063   650-369-4230
5945 Balboa Avenue, San Diego, CA 92111   858-565-9181

FLORIDA
145 S.W. 107th Avenue, Miami, FL 33174   305-559-6715

HAWAII
1143 Bishop Street, Honolulu, HI 96813   808-521-2731
Neighbor Islands call: 866-521-2731

ILLINOIS
172 North Michigan Avenue, Chicago, IL 60601   312-346-4228

LOUISIANA
4403 Veterans Memorial Blvd, Metairie, LA 70006   504-887-7631

MASSACHUSETTS
885 Providence Hwy, Dedham, MA 02026   781-326-5385

MISSOURI
9804 Watson Road, St. Louis, MO 63126   314-965-3512

NEW YORK
64 West 38th Street, New York, NY 10018   212-754-1110

PENNSYLVANIA
Philadelphia—relocating   215-969-5068

SOUTH CAROLINA
243 King Street, Charleston, SC 29401   843-577-0175

VIRGINIA
1025 King Street, Alexandria, VA 22314   703-549-3806

CANADA
3022 Dufferin Street, Toronto, ON M6B 3T5   416-781-9131

Saint André Bessette